capoeira

FUSING DANCE AND MARTIAL ARTS

Liz Gogerly

Lerner Publications Company
Minneapolis

First American edition published in 2012 by Lerner Publishing Group, Inc. Published by arrangement with Wayland, a division of Hachette Children's Books

Lerner Publications Company
A division of Lerner Publishing Group, Inc.
241 First Avenue North
Minneapolis, MN U.S.A.

Website address: www.lernerbooks.com

Library of Congress Cataloging-in-Publication Data
Gogerly, Liz.
    Capoeira : fusing dance and martial arts / by Liz Gogerly.
      p.   cm. — (On the radar: dance)
    Includes index.
    ISBN 978-0-7613-7766-5 (lib. bdg. : alk. paper)
    1. Capoeira (Dance)—Juvenile literature. I. Title.
GV1796.C145G64 2012
793.3'1981—dc22   2011002379

Manufactured in the United States of America
1—CG—7/15/11

Photo Acknowledgments
Images in this book are used with the permission of: Dreamstime: Galluccio 17 cr; Flickr: Ben Coombs 7, Alper Çugun 2t, 5; Shutterstock: AJancso 17cr, Arsen 7, Gianluca Curti 10–11, Fanfo 16, Jose Gil 2b, 15tr, Rafael Martin-Gaitero 12–13, 24, Losevsky Pavel 22–23, Maria Weidner 17 tr; Rex: Roger-Viollet 4, Warner Brothers/ Everett Collection 25.

Main body text set in
Helvetica Neue LT Std 13/15.5.
Typeface provided by Adobe Systems.

cover stories

the**people**

the**moves**

the**talk**

SLAVE DANCE

Capoeira (kah-puh-WEE-ruh) may enchant those who watch it, but its original purpose was not to entertain. The sport taught the people who practiced it how to survive and allowed them secretly to keep their culture alive.

Uniting the slaves

Capoeira is believed to have been developed by the Africans who were taken as slaves to Brazil by the Portuguese in the sixteenth century. The slaves were treated badly. Over the years, some slaves escaped and built settlements in Brazil's mountainous forests. Although the slaves came from different countries, they were united in their quest for freedom.

Capoeira and the fight for freedom united slaves from all over Africa.

Jungle war

The Africans developed a form of fighting called jungle war to protect themselves and their settlements. Ex-slaves would go into the plantations and teach this style of fighting to those who were still captive. To avoid suspicion, the ex-slaves introduced music and acrobatic elements to the fighting, leading the slave masters to believe that they were dancing. This fighting to music became known as capoeira. The moves and rules of capoeira are in Portuguese, the language of Brazil.

Capoeira today

When Brazil outlawed slavery in 1850, many former slaves continued to dance. In the harsh conditions on the Brazilian streets, capoeira became associated with gangs and street fights, and it was banned in 1892. The ban was lifted in 1918, and Brazil's first capoeira school opened in 1932. The sport continues to grow. Capoeira schools are in more than 130 countries around the world.

FIGHTING TALK

Know your *ginga* from your *jogo* with our ultimate guide to capoeira lingo!

agogô
an African musical instrument with two hollow wooden cones that are hit to create sound

bateria
the group of musical instruments played at a *jogo*. It may include *pandeiros*, *reco-recos*, and *agogôs*.

aluno
a student of capoeira

berimbau
a musical instrument that looks like a large bow with a hollowed-out gourd attached to the bottom

ginga (swing)
the basic move of capoeira

aluno formado
a capoeirista who is qualified to teach

jogo
a game of capoeira

aluno graduado
a capoeirista who is good enough to show others how to play but who is not qualified to open a school or assist a teacher

boca de calça (hems of the pants)
a capoeira takedown that is executed by grabbing and pulling on the legs of the opponent's pants

macaquinho (little monkey)
an acrobatic escape move that means "little monkey" in Portuguese

atabaque
a large wooden drum

canivete (jackknife)
a capoeira move used to attack or dodge opponents

martelo (hammer)
a lightning-fast kick

aú (cartwheel)
a capoeira move very similar to a cartwheel

capoeirista
someone who plays capoeira

meia lua de frente (half-moon)
a powerful kick in which the player makes a half-moon shape when swinging the leg

cordão
the cord or the belt worn by a capoeirista to denote the person's level of skill

mestre
the highest rank a capoeirista can have

pandeiro

a type of tambourine played as part of the *bateria*

roda

a circle of capoeira players in which *jogos* are played

reco-reco

a musical instrument that is usually made from a section of bamboo with grooves cut into the side. It is played by rubbing a stick over the grooves to make a raspy sound.

takedown

a move in which a player forces the opponent to the floor

pandeiro

GLOSSARY

adrenaline

a hormone found in the human body that causes the heart to beat faster

captive

to be held against your will

choreograph

to create a routine, usually in dancing

enchant

to fascinate and captivate

evade

to get around or avoid

fusion

a mixture of two or more different things

martial art

a combat-based sport that often teaches self-discipline and self-defense rather than aggression

outmaneuver

to move more effectively than someone else

plantations

large farms where crops were grown and harvested by slaves

self-esteem

confidence in and respect for yourself

settlement

a place where a group of people live

spar

an unaggressive fight in which attack and defense moves are practiced

stamina

the ability to do something for a long time

STARTING OUT

My story by Sol "Neve" Berger

My family jokes that I started capoeira before I was even born. When my mom practiced her capoeira moves, I used to somersault inside her tummy! I had to wait until I was three years old before I had my first lesson. Last year, my mom joined a famous capoeira group, and I began to go to classes there every week.

I loved the music. Its strong beat and rhythms really helped me to learn the moves. I was so impressed watching experienced capoeiristas in the roda, and it gave me something to work toward. Very soon, I became more experienced, and my acrobatic moves improved. I was given my capoeira nickname, "Neve," which means *snow*. I learned that capoeira is much more than backflips and kicks. It has made me mentally and physically stronger. I have gained a lot of confidence, and the self-discipline involved in capoeira has helped me with my schoolwork too.

I have met some fantastic people of all ages through capoeira, from young kids and teenagers to older people. My aim is to enter competitions next. I'm not ready yet, but one day I will be. Capoeira has changed my life for sure, and I feel proud to say I'm a capoeirista!

Neve

MUSICAL COMBAT

Capoeira is a spectacular mix of martial arts, acrobatics, music, and dance. It combines graceful leaps, flips, and spins with powerful kicks and takedowns.

How to play

A group of players sits or stands in the roda. Two capoeiristas play the game (*jogo*) in the center of the roda. They do not make contact with each other. Instead, they combine flowing movements to attack and evade each other. Capoeira is a battle of wills and skills, and everyone gets a turn in the middle of the circle. If players take part in a tournament, a panel of judges decides who is the winner. In ordinary jogos, which are not judged, no clear winner may result.

Music and rhythm

Capoeira is always played to music. People in the roda play instruments or chant and clap out rhythms. The music sets the pace of the game and helps players to coordinate their moves. It includes songs sung in Portuguese that are played on the bateria. The bateria includes berimbaus, pandeiros, reco-recos, atabaques, and agogôs.

Capoeira culture

Community and friendship are a huge part of capoeira. People at all levels play together. Experienced graduates help students to learn new moves. Players learn the core values of respect, responsibility, safety, and freedom.

Rules of the roda:

- Make sure you are on time. Punctuality is important in capoeira!
- Avoid gaps in the roda.
- Shake hands with your opponent after your game.
- Respect those capoeiristas who are more experienced than you are.

PULLING RANK

Like other martial arts, capoeira has a ranking system. Capoeiristas work hard over many years to achieve the next grade—and the respect of their fellow capoeiristas.

The student

Once a person starts playing capoeira, he or she is called an aluno, or a student. The student has a baptism (*batizado*), where the student is given a ranking cord or belt to wear around the waist. Sometimes, the student is given a nickname (*apelido*). Usually, the nickname refers to some aspect of a player's character or appearance.

The graduate

When a student is good enough to teach others, he or she becomes a graduate and is called an aluno graduado. While the graduate can teach others how to play, he or she cannot be the main teacher or open a capoeira school.

The teacher

Once a capoeirista is good enough to be an assistant instructor, he or she is called an aluno formado. After several years of training under a capoeira mestre (master), alunos formados can become teachers and then they may run their own capoeira schools.

Master of the sport

Mestre is the highest rank any capoeirista can achieve. A mestre is a teacher who has been given the title of master by others. Usually, the mestre has trained for 15 to 20 years. Mestre Bimba was one of the most well-known masters of capoeira in Brazil. He dedicated himself to capoeira and worked tirelessly when the sport was banned to make it legal again.

DANCE OR FIGHT?

FOR

People who play capoeira believe this fusion of dance and martial arts is a great way to keep the body and mind healthy. They say:

1. The acrobatic moves work every muscle in the body. Players develop agility, strength, and stamina.
2. The sport is a workout for the brain too! You need to outsmart your opponent by being decisive and aware of his or her next move.
3. Capoeira is sociable. Players train in groups, and every game is played inside a circle of people.
4. Capoeira builds self-esteem and good self-defense techniques.
5. Lessons are open to everyone, regardless of age or physical ability. Beginners are encouraged to develop at their own pace.
6. Players do not need expensive gear. Beginners start in sweats, a T-shirt, and bare feet.
7. The rules of capoeira can help people to become more disciplined in their everyday lives.

However, some people think that capoeira is a dangerous martial art based on violent fighting moves. They say:

1. Doing acrobatics on a hard floor is dangerous because people can get thrown, kicked, or knocked down. There is a high risk of injury.
2. It can take several years to train as an instructor. As the sport becomes more popular, some unqualified teachers may set up classes and put students at risk of injuries.
3. Capoeira classes can appear to be closed to outsiders and joining in can be difficult.
4. The capoeira culture draws people in and can take over their lives much more than other types of martial arts.
5. Players can start to feel aggressive, and real fights have been known to break out inside the roda.

AGAINST

Right or wrong?

Like all martial arts, capoeira is a great way to exercise and to learn new skills. It allows players to enjoy the competition and energy of combat without any physical contact. Capoeira is safe as long as it is carried out with proper guidance and training.

15

CAPOEIRA STYLE

Capoeira is fast and free-flowing, so loose, comfortable clothes are important. Beginners can start in simple sweats and a T-shirt.

Classic whites

Many capoeiristas wear white. This tradition was formalized by Mestre Bimba, who set up the world's first official capoeira school in Bahia, Brazil. Students wore white uniforms to show that capoeira was about respect and discipline and not about gangs and fighting.

In uniform

Most capoeira groups have their own uniform, often loose, stretchy white pants (*abadas*) and a shirt. T-shirts are fitted so that they do not fall over a player's head during handstands.

Loose, stretchy pants allow players to perform acrobatic moves.

Feet first

Players go barefoot or wear lightweight, nonslip shoes. Inexperienced capoeiristas may also wear nonslip gloves to help with handstands and cartwheels.

Members of the roda play music with the berimbaus and pandeiros of the bateria.

Accessories

As capoeiristas learn more about the roots of their sport, many wear strings of Brazilian beads that jangle as they play. Some capoeiristas carry their own berimbaus, the stringed instruments played during the dance.

berimbau

Winning belts

Capoeiristas wear cordãos around their waists. As in other martial arts, capoeiristas work toward colored belts that show their rank, or level. The belt colors include white, green, yellow, blue, and purple. Some belts mix colors in braids to indicate progressing skills. It can take years to build the skill, discipline, musical ability, and knowledge needed to earn each new cordão.

THE SWING

The swing (*ginga*) is the basis for all capoeira moves. Get this basic move right, and it's game on!

You will need:

- **floor space** • **bare feet**
- **loose, comfortable clothes**

1

Step to the right. Swing your left leg behind you, putting some weight on it. At the same time, sweep your left arm around in front of you.

2

Bring your left leg forward so that you are standing with your legs apart, knees bent.

3

Move your weight over to your left, and swing your right leg behind you. Sweep your right arm in front of you.

4

Bring your right leg forward so that you are in the same standing position as you were in step 2.

5

Shift your weight to your right leg, and swing your left leg behind you again. Repeat the steps.

Got it?

Ginga means "to swing," and if it is done correctly, you should move from side to side with a swaying motion. The ginga is used in preparation for other, more complicated moves.

MARK "FERRADURA" OBSTFELD

On the Radar talks to Mark "Ferradura" Obstfeld, talented capoeirista at London's Capoeira Academy. Find out why he loves this "beautiful and dangerous" sport.

How did you get into capoeira?

My friend was taught capoeira for his work as an acrobat and stuntman. One day, he showed me some mind-blowing moves. I was so impressed that when I saw a poster advertising capoeira classes, I jumped at the chance.

How has capoeira changed your life?

Capoeira has opened up my world and given me a huge confidence boost. I have met some of my best friends at the academy, and I love training with them. We learn from each other, but there's always that competitive edge too—which keeps things interesting!

Gym workout or capoeira?

Capoeira! I've never been in better shape. My body is toned, I'm flexible, and I have lots of stamina. I could have gone to a gym, but it's great training with others. And if I'm ever in trouble, I know how to defend myself!

Have you had any injuries?

I haven't been badly injured, but accidents can happen if you don't concentrate while your opponent is kicking. The acrobatics are also risky. It's important to train hard and wait until you're ready to take on difficult moves. A good teacher helps you every step of the way.

What does your capoeira name mean?

All capoeira nicknames have some sort of meaning. Mine means "horseshoe." Not because I'm lucky but because the remains of the hair I once had now form a horseshoe shape around the back of my head!

Mark *(left)* spars with a fellow capoeirista.

What is the best way to start capoeira?

Find a school near you, and give it a try! Don't be put off if you see other people speaking to each other in Portuguese and doing amazing moves. Remember, they were beginners once too!

How young can you start?

My first mestre was six when he started capoeira, and I've seen kids of three or four trying it. Anyone who can walk steadily can try capoeira!

THE HEAT

Beats from the berimbau and atabaque fill the air. The rhythms pulse through your body, and all thoughts fade from your mind as you focus on the contest. Your body feels powerful and free under your light clothes. Energized by the anticipation in the air, you move into the roda, clapping and singing with the group. Let the jogo begin!

Lightning speed

A capoeirista cartwheels into the ring, inviting you to spar. You launch yourself into the center, feeling a dizzying rush of air as you flip onto your hands. Then you swoop down into a swaying ginga, concentrating on your next move. Every muscle in your body is tense and ready to burst into action.

Explosive energy

The beat of the music pulses through your body, and a wave of adrenaline surges through your veins. All eyes are fixed on you and your opponent. You focus on her every move, and your body reacts, driven by the energy of the music and the clapping crowd. She comes at you with a wild leg sweep, but you cartwheel out of danger. You roll away to escape a spinning kick and flip into a handstand. Your moves have been nearly perfect, and she can't get close.

Eye to eye

As the jogo ends, you look your partner in the eye. You were graceful and powerful. She backs out of the roda with a nod of respect. You feel so alive and ready to take on anything. When you have played the game well, there is no feeling that touches it.

LIGHTS, CAMERA, CAPOEIRA!

A new martial arts craze is sweeping the world. Capoeira blends high-energy fighting skills with mesmerizing dance moves. It is springing up everywhere from Hollywood films to television ads. What makes it so popular?

Hollywood style

Capoeiristas can choreograph impressive fight scenes, without injuries or special effects. No wonder they're in demand with filmmakers! Capoeira's elegant flips and kicks made it the obvious choice for Halle Berry's role in *Catwoman* (2004). The actress trained with a top mestre before shooting her fight scenes.

Capoeria has also worked its magic in *Harry Potter and the Goblet of Fire* (2005). The sport's high-energy moves showcased the amazing strength and agility of the Durmstrang pupils. But in the movies, the opponent is not always another person! A thief in *Ocean's Twelve* (2004), for example, used capoeira moves to outmaneuver a laser security system.

Capoeira fever!

The public has gone capoeira crazy. The Afro-Brazilian sport is spicing up parties, concerts, and awards shows all over the world. Capoeira moves are music video scene-stealers, and capoeirista clips get millions of hits online. So get out there and find a class to see what the fuss is all about!

In its native Brazil, capoeira is practiced by many very young children.

"Capoeira is probably the hardest thing on the planet to learn to do," says Halle Berry. "And I had to learn how to do everything in high heels!"

THE HALF-MOON

This *meia lua de frente* gets its name from the half circle drawn by the kicking leg.

You will need:

- floor space   • bare feet
- loose, comfortable clothes

1 Start with a basic swing move.

2 Step out of the swing on your left foot, lifting your right leg to the side and up as you do so.

3

Continue to swing your leg around in a half-moon shape in front of your body. Try to lift your leg up high, but take care not to fall over!

5

Step back on your right leg, crouching slightly as you land your foot, and get ready for your next move.

4

Bring your leg across your body and down to the left. Twist your body to the right to keep your balance.

Got it?

Your right leg should have made a half circle in front of your body. You should have kept your body steady and used your arms for balance by moving them in the opposite direction to the swing of your leg.

27

THE MOVES

hems of the pants

jackknife

cartwheel

little monkey

hammer

Players try to outsmart their opponent with leg sweeps, takedowns, and kicks. At the same time, they defend themselves with dynamic acrobatics, rolls, and ducks. The goal is to perform the moves well without making physical contact.

jackknife (*canivete*)

This is a clever move used for attack or defense. Players fool the opponent into moving close so the player can deliver an unexpected kick or strike.

hems of the pants (*boca de calça*)

This amazing takedown is performed by pulling the opponent's leg from underneath the opponent as the other leg passes above the player's head.

cartwheel (*aú*)

This defensive move is used by a player to spin away from an attacking opponent.

little monkey (*macaquinho*)

This nifty ground move allows the player to move quickly out of danger. Players keep the upper body facing forward as they roll the legs backward from a crouching position.

hammer (*martelo*)

In this fast-moving strike, the player kicks one foot at the opponent—aiming for the head—while keeping the other foot on the ground. The shin or instep of the foot can be used to land this kick.

THE HAMMER

Start with a basic swing move. From this move, step forward on your left foot.

2

The martelo kick is fast and furious!

You will need:

- floor space • bare feet
- loose, comfortable clothes

Move your weight onto your left foot, and as you do so, lift your right leg, with your knee bent.

3

Quickly extend your leg and kick it up to head height. Put your arm up to protect your face. (If you were using this move while sparring, you would be prepared for your opponent's counterattack.)

4

Bring your leg back down. Use your arms to steady yourself, and then continue the swing.

Got it?

You should have swung the leg and delivered your kick with maximum power. To defend yourself from a counterattack after a hammer, you should hold your arms in front of your face.

31

GET MORE INFO

Books & DVDs

Ancona, George. *Capoeira: Game! Dance! Martial Art!* New York: Lee & Low Books, 2007. Colorful, action-packed photos show capoeiristas in Brazil and the United States playing the game.

Brazilian Capoeira for Beginners. Hollywood, CA: Rising Sun Productions, 2001. This DVD, filmed in Brazil with a master and his students, gives instruction on the basic techniques.

Capoeira: Instruction and Demonstrations. Playasound, 2007. This DVD gives basic instruction as well as some history of the music and the sport.

Capoeira: The Dance of Freedom. Salt Lake City: University of Utah, 2005. This DVD documentary by Steve Bartholomew explores the culture that brought capoeira to life.

Haney, Johannah. *Capoeira*. Tarrytown, NY: Marshall Cavendish, 2011. This book shows capoeristas in action.

Websites

Capoeira Arts
http://www.capoeiraarts.com/
This website is part of the Capoeira Arts Foundation, whose mission is to promote capoeira as an art form. The website has music, clothing, instructional DVDs, and links to schools.

Virtual Capoeira
http://www.virtualcapoeira.com/
This website provides links to local schools, a calendar of events, and a background on the sport.

INDEX